M000013678

PRINCIPLES,

PROMISES,

& POWER

Possessing Your Inheritance

WILLIAM V. THOMPSON

© Copyright 1998 — William V. Thompson

All rights reserved. This book is protected under the copyright laws of the United States of America. This book may not be copied or reprinted for commercial gain or profit. The use of short quotations or occasional page copying for personal or group study is permitted and encouraged. Permission will be granted upon request. Unless otherwise identified, Scripture quotations are from the King James Version of the Bible. Scripture quotations marked (TLB) are taken from The Living Bible © 1971. Used by permission of Tyndale House Publishers, Inc., Wheaton, IL 60189. All rights reserved. Scripture quotations marked (RSV) are taken from the Revised Standard Version and those marked (TEV) are taken from Today's English Version. All emphasis within Scripture quotes is the author's own.

Take note that the name satan and related names are not capitalized. We choose not to acknowledge him, even to the point of violating grammatical rules.

Treasure House

An Imprint of
Destiny Image® Publishers, Inc.
P.O. Box 310
Shippensburg, PA 17257-0310

"For where your treasure is,
there will your heart be also." Matthew 6:21

ISBN 1-56043-308-6

For Worldwide Distribution
Printed in the U.S.A.

This book and all other Destiny Image, Revival Press
and Treasure House books are available
at Christian bookstores and distributors worldwide.

For a U.S. bookstore nearest you, call **1-800-722-6774**.
For more information on foreign distributors, call **717-532-3040**.
Or reach us on the Internet: **http://www.reapernet.com**

Dedication

This book is dedicated to my beautiful, wonderful wife, Joy, who supports and encourages me. She has challenged me not only to dream dreams but also to fulfill them. This book is truly a dream come true.

Acknowledgments

When you have lived as much of this material as we have, writing a book like this is simply a by-product of our life, with its various financial seasons. I wish to thank all those persons who have inspired me in writing this book.

To my mother, who raised me to believe that if it can be done, then I *can* do it through Christ.

To my pastor, Dr. Otis Lockett, Sr., who labors in the Word, who challenged me to strive for excellence, and who birthed in me an entrepreneurial spirit.

And to my friend, Fatin Horton, whose dedication and development of insightful ideas is priceless.

Introduction

Principles, promises, and power—three of the main ingredients of the Kingdom of God. Our level of understanding in these three areas will greatly influence our level of success in the Kingdom. Since Adam, God has given man sovereign promises to stand on and the power to receive, possess, and maintain His blessing. However, problems set in when God's principle is missed.

For every promise, there is a principle that leads to a provision. Church history is filled with people who have claimed the promises of God but missed the blessing because they missed the eternal principle and therefore were not empowered to walk in the provision. God has promised that "the wealth of the sinner is laid up for the just," (Prov. 13:22b), that if we pay our tithes and offerings He will pour out a blessing for which there will not be room enough to receive it (see Mal. 3:10), and that if we give, it will be given unto us (see Lk. 6:38)—and God cannot lie (see Num. 23:19). Yet, countless Christians live in poverty and die broke. We understand the promises and benefits that come from giving, but we miss the principles of sowing and reaping.

The New Testament is a manifestation of promise, but it was first taught in the Old Testament as principle. The promise of the Messiah was manifested out of the principle of sacrifice. Hosea 4:6 says that the lack of knowledge destroys not because it is not available, but because it is rejected. If we are honest, we will admit that money is one issue that has become taboo in our churches. Yet, addressing it is one of our greatest needs.

In Matthew 25:14-30, a parable is told of three men who were given the responsibilities of stewardship by their master. Verse 15 of that passage clearly states that the talents were given to the men based on their ability. Therefore, we see that God gives us only what we are able to effectively handle. When understanding and ability increase, so does our stewardship

This brings us to the purpose of this book: God has given me 105 principles birthed from the Word of God that directly relate to *your* personal finances. My prayer is that understanding and application will come to the Church, so that we can take back from the devil all the wealth God has laid up for us (see Prov. 13:22). Through this, the Kingdom of God will be further established, and we will be empowered to effectively occupy until He comes (see Lk. 19:13)!

Principles for Personal Finances

Appendices

Principle #1

"God wants to take what you have to create what you need."

Promise

And Elisha said unto her, What shall I do for thee? tell me, what hast thou in the house? And she said, Thine hand-maid hath not any thing in the house, save a pot of oil. ... And he said, Go, sell the oil, and pay thy debt, and live thou and thy children of the rest (2 Kings 4:2,7b).

Power

Often people overlook sources of potential income because they are not in money form. Yet the things that we are overlooking may be God's answer in our current situation. God did not promise us the power to get money; He promised us the power to get wealth. *Wealth* is anything with the potential to create re-sources to complete the will of God and provide for our needs. In Second Kings, God took the single pot of oil that the widow had and expanded it into what she needed. Most of us overlook our "pot of oil." We feel that it is insignificant for solving our problems. Some examples of a "pot of oil" are:

1. Bills: Our Ten-Ten Theory says that everyone has at least ten expenses. Reduce ten expenses by $10 each for $100 of newfound income. (See Appendix A.)

2. Talents: Everyone possesses a talent that can make them money (e.g., bookkeeping, typing, tutoring, yard work, car detailing, baby-sitting, etc.). Tap your talent for cash. Even consider

bartering, exchanging your talents for the talents of another, to meet your needs.

3. Tax Refund: This option may have two possibilities. First, if you receive a refund, you can adjust your withholdings to get the refund in your paycheck. (Form W-4 allows you to change allowances.) Second, develop tax strategies to increase your refund, since your current refund represents only a small amount of what was withheld. Find ways to get the most back. (See Appendix B.)

4. Company Benefits: Many benefits, like 401k plans, provide tax savings *and* make you money, since your company will match some or all of your contributions.

5. Overtime: Request overtime and use the extra money to attack debt.

Principle #2

"Money flows into our lives based on the size of our cistern (vessel)."

Promise

And it came to pass, when the vessels were full, that she said unto her son, Bring me yet a vessel. And he said unto her, There is not a vessel more. And the oil stayed (2 Kings 4:6).

Power

God gives to us in proportion to our ability to handle His gifts. The woman asked her son for another jar because she was expecting more oil. However, the flow stopped because God knew that she had run out of jars and could handle no more, even though He had more to give. God assesses our ability to manage money; the greater the ability, the greater the inflow. The amount of money that you currently have is based on God's assessment of your ability! God is able to pour money into our lives, but we lack the ability to manage it. Consider this: Although you love your child, what keeps you from giving him or her $10,000 (if you have it)? It's their inability to handle the money. The best way to enhance your ability to manage money is to show God that you can handle it according to the principles found in *His* Word. If God can *trust* you, then He'll *entrust* you!

Principle #3

"You will always know what God has given you by how hard it is to keep it."

Promise

The blessing of the Lord, it maketh rich, and He addeth no sorrow with it (Proverbs 10:22).

Power

If you're struggling to keep something (a house, a car, a credit card, etc.), you may need to consider that perhaps God never authorized you to obtain it. Anytime we go out and purchase something that God has not authorized, He has no obligation to help us pay for it. However, if God authorizes a purchase, it becomes His responsibility, and there is no struggle to keep it.

Principle #4

"First things first lifts the spending curse."

Promise

Honour the Lord with thy substance, and with the ***firstfruits*** *of all thine increase: So shall thy barns be filled with plenty, and thy presses shall burst out with new wine* (Proverbs 3:9-10).

Power

"Priority Spending" says that your *first* financial priority is to pay your tithe and give your offering. Because so many believers spend God's money without proper reverence and consideration to tithing, their spending is placed under a curse, and consequently, the items that were bought are also cursed. A cursed item cannot fulfill the purpose for which it was purchased. Your *second* priority should be your bills and necessary living expenses (see Prov. 3:27). Your *third* priority should be your savings and sacrificial offerings (see Prov. 21:20 TLB). Non-necessities and wants should fall into *fourth* and *fifth* place! Top priorities should always come first! This is how we honor God with our substance.

Wisdom note: Savings (third priority) should come before eating out, movies, cable TV, clothes (non-work), cellular phone, CDs, tapes, travel, etc. These are all fourth and fifth priority items! (See Appendix C.)

Principle #5

"Bargains seldom come with a brand name attached."

Promise

"Utterly worthless!" says the buyer as he haggles over the price. But afterwards he brags about his bargain! (Proverbs 20:14 TLB)

Power

The goal of every person should always be to find the best quality items at the lowest price. However, many individuals have the misconception that if the item does not have a brand name or a trademark symbol, then it's not top quality. Realize that most name brand items are sold under "unbranded" or store labels for substantially less money, yet they have the same quality. Finding bargains means there will be more money to attack debt, to save, or to advance the Kingdom. Hot brand names are like the heavens and the earth; they are destined to pass away.

Principle #6

"God hates when you build a house using someone else's blueprints."

Promise

Neither shalt thou desire thy neighbour's wife, neither shalt thou covet thy neighbour's house, his field, or his manservant, or his maidservant, his ox, or his ass, or anything that is thy neighbour's (Deuteronomy 5:21).

Power

God has designed a special plan, a "blueprint," for the life of each person. However, when you look at your neighbor's possessions to determine your desires, you hinder God from working His plan of action in your life. Hunger for God's plan for your life and seek to understand what you should ask of Him. Don't try to imitate or compare yourself with others. Even though your friend may have just bought a new car, you should not feel obligated to do the same, for you don't know the costs (e.g. loss of peace, no money for emergencies) that may be attached to the purchase. Set your own financial goals and establish timetables for achieving them. Be driven by God's plan for your desires, not by the desires and actions of others. Scripture declares that comparing yourself to another is not wise (see 2 Cor. 10:12). Let the Word of God be the ruler by which you measure yourself.

Principle #7

"Welfare reform starts at the offering plate."

Promise

For the poor shall never cease out of the land: therefore I command thee, saying, Thou shalt open thine hand wide unto thy brother, to thy poor, and to thy needy, in thy land (Deuteronomy 15:11).

Power

Due to the changes in the economic cycle that are expected over the next few years, the Church must assume its responsibility of providing help for the needy. Welfare, based on the Bible, is not the *government's* responsibility, but the *Church's*. Therefore, every member of the Church must position him or herself to financially assume this responsibility. After all, you can't help others if you need help yourself. Welfare is currently being reformed, and soon there may be no welfare at all. If the Church is not in position to help people, the day will come when the needy will have no hope.

If you want to get out of poverty, the offering plate is the best place for you to make a deposit. Jesus taught us, "Give, and it shall be given unto you" (Lk. 6:38a). His promise was not made contingent upon the economy.

Principle #8

"Insanity is knowing how much you make and spending more than that."

Promise

Much food is in the tillage of the poor: but there is that is destroyed for want of judgment (Proverbs 13:23).

Power

Often times people complain that they don't make enough. However, the problem is usually that they *spend more than they make*. In most cases, people make enough money to handle their everyday expenses, but through credit abuse, greed, or lack of discipline, their expenses exceed their income. Most people have the *resources* to live a comfortable life with all their basic needs met; however, they try to live based upon society, the vantage points of others, or the desires of their flesh, and they neglect the guidelines of the Word. Most people don't have a *money* problem; they have a *management* problem that has led to a *money* problem. Remember, in most cases your income came before your bills.

Principle #9

"Pride keeps the financially crippled in a wheelchair."

Promise

Pride goeth before destruction, and an haughty spirit before a fall (Proverbs 16:18).

Power

Can a drowning man save himself? No! Therefore, it should be obvious to you that, if your finances are in poor shape, and have been for some time, you need some help to get them in order. If you can correct the problem yourself, why haven't you? If you have trouble understanding finances, go to someone who does. If not, destruction shall surely overtake *you and your family*. There is no reason for believers to struggle financially, for God has given revelation and financial wisdom to saints in just about every local body. Someone is available to help you. Asking for help is not a sign of weakness, but of wisdom. Unstrap the ankle straps of pride so that you will no longer be bound to the "wheelchair" of poor finances.

Principle #10

"People thirst for money without really tapping their wells."

Promise

Much food *is in the tillage of the* **poor**: *but there is that is destroyed for want of judgment* (Proverbs 13:23).

Power

Most people long for more money but have not fully tapped the resources that God has already given them! Things such as company benefits, tax refunds, talents, unused assets, and overtime are only a few of the items that your "well" may contain to help enhance your present financial condition. (See Appendix D.) *Never try to tap someone else's well without first tapping your own.*

Principle #11

"An unwritten plan is impossible to follow."

Promise

And the Lord answered me, and said, Write the vision, and make it plain upon tables, that he may run that readeth it (Habakkuk 2:2).

Power

The purpose of a written financial plan is to outline *exactly* what you want to accomplish, detailing step by step how you will achieve it. A written plan keeps you on track with your goals and gives you and your spouse/covenant partner a point of agreement. Your partner will be able to follow you because he or she understands where you're headed and how you will get there. Without a written plan, you'll wander in the wilderness all your life without ever experiencing the promised land. This plan should be the standard against which all your actions are measured to make sure that you're headed in the right direction.

Principle #12

"Broken vows look a lot like past due bills."

Promise

Better is it that thou shouldest not vow, than that thou shouldest vow and not pay (Ecclesiastes 5:5).

Power

Whenever something is bought on credit, you have made a vow to the vendor to repay that money at a specific time. This vow should be kept as if it was made to God. Some things can only be decreed and established in prayer after your vow has been fulfilled (see Job 22:27-28). If people can't trust your word in business, then they won't trust your word about Jesus!

Principle #13

"Debt: A contagious disease that contaminates the whole family."

Promise

Now there cried a certain woman of the wives of the sons of the prophets unto Elisha, saying, Thy servant my husband is dead; and thou knowest that thy servant did fear the Lord: **and the creditor is come to take unto him my two sons to be bondmen** (2 Kings 4:1).

Power

Debt affects every member of your family! Its contagious force is so great that it will impact your immediate family, your extended family, and even generations to come. A spouse's frustration because of debt can cause conflicts in the marriage, which can spill over to the children and cause turmoil throughout the house. Since children follow the examples of their parents, they too will adopt a lifestyle of living from paycheck to paycheck and of dodging creditors. Ask yourself the question, "Where did I learn my financial habits?" *Debt has one purpose—to kill.* Debt kills families, friendships, self-esteem, vision, relationships, health, even entire lives. (See Appendix E.)

Principle #14

"Savings is the bill that almost everyone is delinquent in paying."

Promise

The wise man saves for the future, but the foolish man spends whatever he gets (Proverbs 21:20 TLB).

Power

Savings should be viewed as a bill to yourself that must be paid each month, not a luxury to enjoy if there is money left over. "Priority Spending" says that your first priority must be your tithe and offerings; second, are your bills and necessary living expenses, and *third, before luxuries*, must be *savings*. Most Christians waste enough money on a weekly basis to easily start a consistent savings plan. The amount you are saving may not be large, but remember that everything starts small—except God! Some basic ways to have money to save include the following:

1. Take your lunch to work.
2. Don't eat out as much.
3. Eliminate unnecessary options on your phone and television.
4. Balance your checkbook to eliminate non-sufficient-funds charges.
5. Locate phone companies that have the lowest rates and six-second-interval billing.

These suggestions are part of our Ten-Ten theory, which requires you to identify ten ways you spend money and then find ways to reduce each of them by $10 a month, for a total savings per month of $100.

Also, save 50 percent of all raises, overtime, or tax refund checks. In order to be successful in saving, you must establish a reason to save.

Wisdom Note: Have your savings automatically drafted from your account like you would a bill (it's a bill to yourself) and make your savings difficult to withdraw (e.g., require two signatures). (See Appendix D.)

Principle #15

"Your faith will work; but it won't work *for* you."

Promise

What doth it profit, my brethren, though a man say he hath faith, and have not works? can faith save him? ... Even so faith, if it hath not works, is dead, being alone (James 2:14,17).

Power

"Works" are the fire that fuels faith, for you will do what you believe! Christians often try to get their faith to do what is meant to be accomplished through work. *Faith* is designed to do what you *can't* do (supernatural); *work* is designed to do what you *can* do (natural). Work includes looking for and working at a job, paying bills, following a budget, balancing your checkbook, and locating bargains. Faith is only activated after the appropriate work has been completed as you attempt to solve a financial matter. God will never do for you what you can do for yourself. Faith works, but it's activated by work.

Principle #16

"Buried dreams contain hidden treasures."

Promise

Again, the kingdom of heaven is like unto treasure hid in a field; the which when a man hath found, he hideth, and for joy thereof goeth and selleth all that he hath, and buyeth that field (Matthew 13:44).

Power

Almost everyone has dreamed something big at one point in his or her life. You may have gathered information, attended workshops, or wanted to start your own business. However, as soon as obstacles arose, you gave up and buried your dreams. *Your buried dreams could contain your financial miracle!* The dream to start a business, return to school, get out of debt, or own a home can be done—just do it! Dig up the dream and look for the hidden treasure that you missed the first time. Someone else may see what you can't. Remember, if God put it in your heart, He's also willing to put it in your hand.

Principle #17

"The reason that God didn't accept Cain's sacrifice was probably because he owed on his Visa."

Promise

The sacrifice of the wicked is an abomination to the Lord (Proverbs 15:8a).

Power

After you have given God your tithe and offerings, your next obligation is to pay your bills (see Prov. 3:27). You cannot take your bill money, give it to God as a *sacrificial* offering, and then try to use your faith to cause God to meet your need. This type of sacrifice is unacceptable to God due to the blemish of your unpaid bill. God does not view that money as yours, but as your creditor's. A biblical sacrifice is when *you*, not your creditors, make the sacrifice. Refraining from eating out, buying clothes, using cable TV and cellular phones, or spending money on entertainment are the kinds of sacrifices that move God.

Principle #18

"Relationships are the currents that determine the direction of your travel."

Promise

Iron sharpeneth iron; so a man sharpeneth the countenance of his friend (Proverbs 27:17).

Power

When you are trying to get your finances in order, accountability is essential. It is important that you create an "environment of change" with people who will challenge you to be the best you can be. The best supporting cast is comprised of people who are striving to be successful and do not mind working and sacrificing for it. Be open to other people's ideas and suggestions; however, keep your ultimate goal in mind. You become like those who surround you; association breeds assimilation. Remember, relationships are like elevators: They will either carry you up or take you down.

Principle #19

"God has the right to disconnect His services to those who are delinquent in payments."

Promise

Will a man rob God? Yet ye have robbed Me. But ye say, Wherein have we robbed Thee? In tithes and offerings. Ye are cursed with a curse: for ye have robbed Me, even this whole nation (Malachi 3:8-9).

Power

What happens if you fail to pay your phone or other utility bill? The service gets disconnected. God, in His mercy, does not disconnect all His services if we fail to pay our tithe and offering. For example, He allows us to keep our life and our salvation. However, He does disconnect the protection plan that rebukes the "devourer" (see Mal. 3:11), which makes us more vulnerable to the attack of the devil in our finances (e.g., loss of job, sickness, no promotion or raise, etc.). Pay your back tithes and the reconnection fee of 20 percent of these unpaid tithes (see Lev. 27:30-31) *now* to get reconnected to God's full service plan.

Principle #20

"When making financial decisions, your *first* step should be a *second* opinion."

Promise

The good man asks for advice from friends; the wicked plunge ahead—and fall (Proverbs 12:26 TLB).

Power

Wise counsel provides insight into tomorrow while planning today. It allows you to be forewarned of the potential pitfalls so that you can develop a plan of attack before you encounter them. By obtaining wise counsel, you are not saying, "Tell me what to do," but "Share your insight, wisdom, knowledge, and experience with me so that I can make the right decision." Obtaining counsel will not eliminate all the mistakes you will make, but it will greatly reduce the number of mistakes and the amount of loss.

Principle #21

"The presence of excuses always destroys the power of potential."

Promise

And [he] *sent his servant at supper time to say to them that were bidden, Come; for all things are now ready. And they all with one consent began to make excuse. … So that servant came, and showed his lord these things. … And the lord said unto the servant, Go out into the highways and hedges, and compel them to come in, that my house may be filled. For I say unto you, That none of those men which were bidden shall taste of my supper* (Luke 14:17-18a,21a,23-24).

Power

You will never move beyond your excuses! You face your biggest enemy when you make excuses for not tapping your full potential. Many times Christians attempt to "spiritualize" their excuses by saying "it's not the timing or the will of God" or "I don't feel led by the Spirit"! God will back anything that you do with the intention of advancing His Kingdom! The only thing that will destroy your potential is your inability to try.

Principle #22

"The picture of success is first developed in the darkroom of your mind."

Promise

For as he thinketh in his heart, so is he... (Proverbs 23:7).

Power

Every action starts as a thought. If you don't think it, you can't do it. The first step to becoming financially successful is to see yourself that way. Picture yourself being free, saving every payday, or paying your bills on time. It is your *attitude* (what you think), which affects your *aspirations* (what you want), which affects your *actions* (what you do), that affects your *accomplishments*! Imagine yourself debt free and never forget that feeling.

Principle #23

"Most people see the big picture but refuse to prepare the blueprints."

Promise

Keep your eyes on Jesus, our leader and instructor. He was willing to die a shameful death on the cross because of the joy He knew would be His afterwards... (Hebrews 12:2 TLB).

Power

Most people can see the big picture, or financial goal, of being debt free or having more than enough, but they are not willing to develop the specific details to achieve the big picture. The tedious work is the blueprints, which require precision, forethought, organization, and a systematic approach to ensure that everything flows and works together. Without a blueprint there can be no house, business, car, or financial success. Financial blueprints look a lot like this:

1. Budgeting
2. Goals and objectives
3. Debt reduction plans
4. Credit rebuilding plans
5. Strategies to cut costs
6. Ideas to increase income
7. Understanding company benefits
8. Tax planning
9. Reviewing investment/retirement options
10. Learning biblical principles for managing money.

Principle #24

"God requires the 'firstfruits'; He does not like 'leftovers'."

Promise

*Honour the Lord with thy substance, with the **firstfruits** of all thine increase: So shall thy barns be filled with plenty, and thy presses shall burst out with new wine* (Proverbs 3:9-10).

Power

The only offering that activates God's promise to fill our barns is that which is given to Him first. The attitude that says, "I'll give to God after I pay my bills, buy myself something, or take care of a few things," disqualifies you from having your barns filled by God. God is honored only when He receives the firstfruits; leftovers are an insult.

Principle #25

"Contentment is knowing how to control your spending when you can't control your income."

Promise

Not that I speak in respect of want: for I have learned, in whatsoever state I am, therewith to be content. I know both how to be abased, and I know how to abound: every where and in all things I am instructed both to be full and to be hungry, both to abound and to suffer need (Philippians 4:11-12).

Power

You have more control over what you spend than what you make. Controlling your spending is like creating income. Being discontented causes you to spend your future income on your present desires. *Contentment is not learning to do without; it is learning to do without something new.* It's not that people don't have. They just aren't content with what they have. Therefore, they desire new things. Most people have all they need to live a comfortable life that is within their means, but few have learned the art of contentment so as to not rob themselves of their future. (See Appendix G.)

Principle #26

"If God knows that you'll sow, He'll always provide seed."

Promise

For God, who gives seed to the farmer to plant, and later on, good crops to harvest and eat, will give you more and more seed to plant and will make it grow so that you can give away more and more fruit from your harvest (2 Corinthians 9:10 TLB).

Power

Giving is a sign to God that you trust Him and that you understand that money is to be seed that is sown. Providing the seed is God's responsibility; sowing is yours. As long as you have a willingness to sow, God will provide the necessary seed because He's called you to be a sower. Remember, as every harvest grows bigger, there will be more for you to sow, more for you to use to help others, and more for you to keep and enjoy!

Principle #27

"Family values are the womb from which financial goals are birthed."

Promise

For where your treasure is, there will your heart be also (Luke 12:34).

Power

Before you can successfully develop your family's financial goals, you must first decide what you value. Things that are important to your family will shape and give birth to your goals. Values and goals must be consistent. *Values birth goals; goals control spending.* Here are some examples from my wife, Joy, and me:

Value	Goal	Spending
• Time together	• Joy working with me	• Keep all bills and living expenses within my income so that Joy's income is not needed
• Minimal financial pressure	• Don't use credit cards	• Pay cash for purchases or wait
• Eating out	• Eat out at least once a week	• Don't waste money on clothes that aren't as important to us

Principle #28

"Goals are the anchors that keep you from being swept away by the winds of overspending."

Promise

Where there is no vision, the people perish: but he that keepeth the law, happy is he (Proverbs 29:18).

Power

What keeps and restrains people from spending everything? Goals! Without goals we run wild in our spending, thus chasing our desires, which leads to *"broke*ness" (not *broken*ness!). Goals give us a reason to say no because there are things in the future that we want more than present gratification. In order for goals to help control our spending, they must have the following qualities:

1. Specific: They must be precise and to the point, detailing exactly what you're trying to accomplish.
2. Meaningful: They must be important enough to make sacrifices for.
3. Measurable: They must be written down and be significant enough to measure progress.
4. Motivational: They must get you excited and pumped up.

What are some financial goals that can help you control your spending?

Principle #29

"The traveling companion of debt is depression."

Promise

About this time there was a great cry of protest from parents against some of the rich Jews who were profiteering on them. What was happening was that families who ran out of money for food had to sell their children or mortgage their fields, vineyards, and homes to these rich men; and some couldn't even do that, for they already had borrowed to the limit to pay their taxes. "We are their brothers and our children are just like theirs," the people protested. "Yet we must sell our children into slavery to get enough money to live. We have already sold some of our daughters, and we are helpless to redeem them, for our fields, too, are mortgaged to these men" (Nehemiah 5:1-5 TLB).

Power

Debt not only brings bills; it also brings depression. The real power of debt is not the bills, but the spirit of depression that the bills bring, creating a sense of hopelessness. Defeat debt, and the depression that you struggle with will flee.

Principle #30

"When finances are divided, it is likely that the house is also."

Promise

And Jesus knew their thoughts, and said unto them, Every kingdom divided against itself is brought to desolation; and every city or house divided against itself shall not stand (Matthew 12:25).

Power

Whenever couples are divided in their finances, financial ruin is soon to follow. Division comes when there are separate checkbooks, savings accounts, bills, debts, budgets, etc., and destruction soon follows. *You will never reach your full financial potential until the two members of a marriage become one* (see Eccles. 4:9). Do you, by working separately, have the assurance that God will be in the midst of your finances (see Mt. 18:19)? How marriage partners handle their finances should reflect the image of God. The Father, the Son, and the Holy Spirit are one; they never operate independently of one another. Neither should the finances of one spouse operate independently of the other. Allow the Word of God to be the final rule and authority that governs your finances—not your feelings, your opinions, or the opinions of others. Allow the Word to discipline your financial philosophy so that you and your spouse can have "all things common."

Principle #31

"God is only obligated to pay for what He authorizes."

Promise

And said unto them, Go ye also into the vineyard, and whatsoever is right I will give you. And they went their way (Matthew 20:4).

Power

God is a responsible God; therefore, anything that He authorizes you to buy, He will take full responsibility for providing the resources necessary to maintain it. If, however, the provided resources are misused, the responsibility is yours again. When you make purchases in His name without His approval, you become liable and responsible for the repayment. Most of the time when people struggle to keep or pay for something, it's a sign of an unauthorized purchase that they are now trying to pay for out of their own resources.

Principle #32

"With every debt that you defeat, your army should get larger."

Promise

If he be able to fight with me, and to kill me, then will we be your servants: but if I prevail against him, and kill him, then shall ye be our servants, and serve us (1 Samuel 17:9).

Power

You've declared war on debt because it is your enemy. The plan of attack to destroy debt follows this general strategy:

1. See debt as an enemy.
2. Stop spending (cash or credit).
3. List your bills smallest to largest. (Remember that David fought the lion and bear before he fought Goliath.)
4. Identify the weapons that you will use to fight the enemy (e.g., overtime, tax refund check, Ten-Ten theory).
5. Attack the smallest debt until it's destroyed. The extra money now becomes a weapon to attack the next largest debt. Every debt that you destroy provides you with extra money, which means a new weapon.

God won't provide you with new weapons if all you are doing is *talking* about attacking debt. (See Appendix E.)

Principle #33

"A vision is the well from which financial discipline is drawn."

Promise

Where there is no vision, the people perish: but he that keepeth the law, happy is he (Proverbs 29:18).

Power

When there is no financial vision, there is no reason for financial discipline. However, once your vision is clearly defined, you will know what you want and what must be done to obtain it. Before you spend, make sure that your spending will help you to fulfill your vision (called "Purpose Spending"). If it doesn't, don't spend. Vision gives you the discipline to say no to spending that has no priority in your life.

Principle #34

"Whenever God sees that you're ready to fight debt, He'll always provide a weapon."

Promise

And the men of Israel said, Have ye seen this man that is come up? surely to defy Israel is he come up: and it shall be, that the man who killeth him, the king will enrich him with great riches, and will give him his daughter, and make his father's house free in Israel. ... And David put his hand in his bag, and took thence a stone, and slang it, and smote the Philistine in his forehead, that the stone sunk into his forehead; and he fell upon his face to the earth (1 Samuel 17:25,49).

Power

Although many say that they want to be debt free, few are willing to show God proof of their sincerity. Things such as developing a budget, cutting spending (e.g., stop using credit cards), listing all bills, and calling your creditors show God that you are able to handle His weapons for attacking debt. For God issues weapons only to those who are ready to fight debt, not to those who are just thinking about it.

Principle #35

"The ability to tolerate your financial situation creates the inability to change it."

Promise

And a certain man was there, which had an infirmity thirty and eight years. When Jesus saw him lie, and knew that he had been now a long time in that case, He saith unto him, Wilt thou be made whole? The impotent man answered Him, Sir, I have no man, when the water is troubled, to put me into the pool: but while I am coming, another steppeth down before me (John 5:5-7).

Power

You can't change your financial situation if you've grown to accept it. The longer you remain in a bad financial situation, the more conditioned to that state you will become. Things that used to bother, frustrate, or anger you won't anymore. What was once a stepping stone (living in an apartment, living from paycheck to paycheck) becomes a place of residence. Eliminating debt becomes not a goal but an impossibility, saving becomes a dream instead of a reality, and the boss continues to be someone else. These are all things you've grown to tolerate; and anything that you've come to tolerate, you won't change.

Principle #36

"Sacrifice is the ability to give up something that you like to obtain something that you love."

Promise

And, behold, one came and said unto Him, Good Master, what good thing shall I do, that I may have eternal life? ... Jesus said unto him, If thou wilt be perfect, go and sell that thou hast, and give to the poor, and thou shalt have treasure in heaven: and come and follow Me (Matthew 19:16,21).

Power

Financial sacrifice is not doing without, but doing without things that you would like to have in order to create revenue for things that you would love to have. Sacrificing is the process of giving up something good for what is the best—those things that you love and that have greater benefit and potential in your life.

Things I Like	Things I Love
• Eating out (often)	• Children's college education fund
• Designer clothes	• Starting your own business
• Cable TV	• Regular vacations
• Expensive cars	• Owning your own house
• Shopping	• Being debt free
• Long distance calls and phone features	• A savings account

Principle #37

"Your credit rating is synonymous with your character rating."

Promise

For when God made a promise to Abraham, because He could swear by no greater, He sware by Himself... (Hebrews 6:13).

Power

Your credit report monitors how faithful you are in keeping your word. Unlike God, many of us give our word to pay a bill by a specific date and don't "watch over our word to perform it" at any cost (see Jer. 1:12 RSV)! Failing to keep your word in paying your bills serves as a reflection of your lack of character. Keep in mind that the reason God's character is enhanced with us is because He keeps His word. (See Appendix H.)

Principle #38

"Your season of saving always precedes your season of spending."

Promise

To every thing there is a season, and a time to every purpose under the heaven: A time to be born, and a time to die; ***a time to plant, and a time to pluck up that which is planted*** (Ecclesiastes 3:1-2).

Power

The laws of nature declare that before you can reap a harvest (a time of spending), there must be a planting of seed (a time of saving). In the realm of finances, the principles remain the same. Before you begin to spend, you must first have a time of saving. The purpose is to bring security to your spending so that you will not face the threat of going into debt (e.g., credit cards) and of not being able to pay your bills. It is your savings that determines how much you can spend; never spend all your savings. Remember, if you haven't entered your season of saving, God has not called you into a season of spending—unless what you are purchasing is a necessity of life.

Principle #39

"Debt: Premature withdrawal from your children's inheritance."

Promise

About this time there was a great cry of protest from parents against some of the rich Jews who were profiteering on them. What was happening was that families who ran out of money for food had to sell their children or mortgage their fields, vineyards, and homes to these rich men; and some couldn't even do that, for they already had borrowed to the limit to pay their taxes. "We are their brothers and our children are just like theirs," the people protested. "Yet we must sell our children into slavery to get enough money to live. We have already sold some of our daughters, and we are helpless to redeem them, for our fields, too, are mortgaged to these men" (Nehemiah 5:1-5 TLB).

Power

God has called every parent to leave enough money for his or her children and "children's children" (see Prov. 13:22). God thinks generationally, but we think in terms of the present. Debt fills your present at the expense of your children's future. By creating debt, you are taking money that God has designed for future generations and using it for your own selfish benefit. All premature withdrawals come with a penalty for disobeying the commandments of God (see Prov. 13:13). The seed that was purposed for your children's future falls victim to the lust of today.

Principle #40

"Excuses are the master locks to the gates of poverty."

Promise

The lazy man is full of excuses. "I can't go to work!" he says. "If I go outside I might meet a lion in the street and be killed!" (Proverbs 22:13 TLB)

Power

Christians have all types of reasons (excuses) why they are not prosperous. Common religious "cover-ups" sound like this:

- "God is trying to teach me something."
- "God is developing me."
- "God wants me to learn to depend on Him."
- "It's not the timing of God."

People make these excuses because it justifies their failures and gives them a reason not to try. If they don't try, no one will ever know what they can do, *including them.* Common excuses can also include these remarks:

- "I don't make enough."
- "Unexpected things always happen."
- "Everyone goes through financially difficult times."
- "I don't know how to manage money."

Consider the impact of excuses in your life. You'll never achieve your God-given greatness if you don't move beyond the excuses that bind you.

Principle #41

"God will never let your sacrifice be a sacrifice to someone else."

Promise

*And He said, Take now **thy** son, thine only son Isaac, whom thou lovest, and get thee into the land of Moriah; and offer him there for a burnt offering upon one of the mountains which I will tell thee of* (Genesis 22:2).

Power

Christians generally have a misconception as to what a sacrificial offering is. Even though you may be in a church service where the minister of God is led of the Spirit to take up a supernatural offering, there are still some biblical guidelines that you must follow in order for your sacrifice to be acceptable to God:

1. You *cannot* give your bill money. This money does not belong to you, but to your creditors. To give it is to break the vow you made to pay the bill on time (see Eccles. 5:4-6). In addition, God has commanded us to pay those that we owe when it is in our power to do it (see Prov. 3:27). Your sacrifice will be blemished because it belongs to someone else.

2. Make a true sacrifice! Acceptable sacrifices would be your hair money, lunch money, clothes money, etc. A true sacrifice is one that is a sacrifice to *you*! (See Appendix F.)

3. Get your finances in order so that the next time there is a sacrificial offering, you'll have extra money to give. The best way to have extra money is to reduce your spending.

Principle #42

"When the potential reward is great, don't be afraid to take the limited risk."

Promise

Keep your eyes on Jesus, our leader and instructor. He was willing to die a shameful death on the cross because of the joy He knew would be His afterwards... (Hebrews 12:2 TLB).

Power

What would you do if you knew that you wouldn't fail? The main hindrance that keeps people from trying something new is the fear of failing. Most things that people desire (e.g., starting a business) cost money; however there is a fear of losing that money. It may cost $5,000 to start a business that could potentially make your dreams come true. The most you could lose is the $5,000 (what you put in); but consider how much you could gain? *This amount is unlimited.* When taking risks, remember that the only thing that's limited is what you can lose.

Principle #43

"Debt's repercussions destroy your seed's reproduction."

Promise

The thief cometh not, but for to steal, and to kill, and to destroy: I am come that they might have life, and that they might have it more abundantly (John 10:10).

Power

Every dollar you have is worth far more than one dollar. It's a seed with the ability to reproduce after its kind. Therefore, when you are plagued by debt, it takes more than your wealth; *it takes your seed and its ability to reproduce*. In the war on debt, your seed is one of your most powerful weapons because of its growth potential.

Principle #44

"It is impossible for the system that impoverishes you to empower you."

Promise

Oh, the joys of those who do not follow evil men's advice, who do not hang around with sinners, scoffing at the things of God: But they delight in doing everything God wants them to, and day and night are always meditating on His laws and thinking about ways to follow Him more closely. They are like trees along a river bank, bearing luscious fruit each season without fail. Their leaves shall never whither, and all they do shall prosper (Psalm 1:1-3 TLB).

Power

There are only two financial systems—the world's and the Word's. Your financial habits in managing money will be shaped and controlled by one of them. The more prevalent system of the two is that of the world, for we are bombarded daily with its philosophy via television, radio, magazines, books, and society. It's even reinforced by Christians who have fallen into the trap of worldly financial systems that were developed generations before and have been passed down. When trying to get out of financial trouble, many turn to the system of the world, which encourages borrowing, paying late, filing bankruptcy, or whatever they think may work. Rarely do we consult the Word of God. We "stand in the way of sinners" when we embrace financial habits without establishing a difference between what is holy and what is unholy (see Ps. 1:1). The world's system has impoverished you; now allow God's system to empower you. If you compare the two systems, you will find the following:

Empowering System (the Word)	Impoverishing System (the World)
• Live within one income (Prov. 31; Tit. 2:3-5).	• Live on both incomes.
• Debt is an enemy (Prov. 22:7).	• Debt is a part of life.
• If you make more money, sow and save more (Eccles. 5:10-11).	• If you make more money, spend more.
• Budgets control cost and eliminate waste (Lk.14:28-30).	• Budgets restrict life.
• Get it before you spend it (Prov. 24:27 TLB).	• Spend it; one day you'll get it.
• Save something every payday (Prov. 21:20 TLB).	• Spend it all.
• Pay your bills on time (Prov. 3:27).	• Pay your bills whenever.

Warning: The two systems cannot be mixed, for the lifestyle of the world and its lusts choke out the Word and keep it from working (see Mk. 4:18-19).

Principle #45

"Financial healing cannot begin until after the 'Plastic Surgery'."

Promise

So the people of Ninevah believed God, and proclaimed a fast, and put on sackcloth, from the greatest of them even to the least of them. ... And God saw their works, that they turned from their evil way; and God repented of the evil, that He had said that He would do unto them; and He did it not (Jonah 3:5,10).

Power

Your first step in getting out of debt is to reduce your spending. The best way to reduce your spending is to cut up *all* credit cards—what we call "Plastic Surgery." Like any major surgery, it's a big decision that requires immediate sacrifice in exchange for a lifetime of benefits. Your road to financial recovery can begin only after the surgery is completed. Remember, credit cards allow you to spend money you don't have on things you don't need to create debt you can't pay!

Principle #46

"Money spent on high fashion can't restore low self-esteem."

Promise

And He said unto them, Take heed, and beware covetousness: for a man's life consisteth not in the abundance of the things which he possesseth (Luke 12:15).

Power

It is impossible to buy enough material things to compensate for low self-esteem. New things are short-term; their effects soon wear off. We adorn ourselves with things, but we never address the real problems. Remember, anything that makes (or attempts to make) God unnecessary is unnecessary! Fashion and its thrill disappear, but the debt created lingers.

Principle #47

**"Goals are the rulers that measure the priority
of our spending."**

Promise

*Where there is no vision, the people perish: but he that
keepeth the law, happy is he* (Proverbs 29:18).

Power

Many of us have financial ambitions, wants, and
desires; however, our spending habits usually don't
reflect those desires. First and foremost, we must establish financial goals to give our money purpose; if
not, we're destined to abuse it. After establishing our
goals, we should then measure every potential purchase or distribution of money against our goals, asking ourselves, "Will this purchase aid me in achieving
my goal?" If the answer is no, then the purchase is not
a priority. By allowing our goals to determine our
spending, it becomes easier and more feasible to determine what we should purchase and what is unnecessary.

Principle #48

"Save it before you see it!"

Promise

He who loves money shall not have enough... The more you have, the more you spend, right up to the limits of your income, so what is the advantage of wealth—except perhaps to watch it as it runs through your fingers! (Ecclesiastes 5:10-11 TLB)

Power

One strategy to avoid the dilemma mentioned in this Scripture is to have your designated savings automatically drafted into your savings account before you "see it" in your check. Within time, you will adjust your spending to the amount of your check. In addition, I recommend that you make it difficult to withdraw this money (i.e., married couples may arrange to require the signature of both spouses to make a withdrawal). Also, before you see your next raise, arrange to have half of that raise automatically drafted into your savings account. This helps to avoid the "I see it; I spend it" syndrome. Imagine the amount of money you would save over the next five to ten years just by saving half of all your raises. Over time, you will begin to view the savings deduction like a bill or a mandatory withholding that you grow to accept as a requirement.

Principle #49

"People try to give more to have more, when they should learn how to have more to give more."

Promise

Jesus said unto him, If thou wilt be perfect, go and sell that thou hast, and give to the poor, and thou shalt have treasure in heaven: and come and follow Me. But when the young man heard that saying, he went away sorrowful: for he had great possessions (Matthew 19:21-22).

Power

Most of us have heard the phrase that "giving is not a loss but a gain" and are familiar with the Scripture "Give, and it shall be given unto you..." (Lk. 6:38). However, we must be careful not to confuse the *promise* that comes with giving with the *purpose* of giving. The *promise* in giving is to give and you will receive more so that you can fulfill the *purpose* of giving, which is to be a blessing to others. Giving should never be used as a means of attaining more material items; it is a medium through which you become a blessing to other people. The rich young man that Jesus was speaking to in Matthew 19 refused to give all that he owned to the poor because he could see no tangible gain that he would receive in return. If he had had the right perspective on giving, he would have seen that he had been blessed so that he could bless other people.

Principle #50

"Small things are just big things that you're not close enough to see."

Promise

He saith unto them, How many loaves have ye? go and see. And when they knew, they say, Five, and two fishes. ... And when He had taken the five loaves and the two fishes, He looked up to heaven, and blessed... And they did all eat, and were filled (Mark 6:38,41a,42).

Power

The seeds of big things are contained inside small things; yet many times they are overlooked because they appear to be so much smaller than our situation. Who, other than Jesus, was close enough to see within the five loaves and two fish the seed that could feed the 5,000? Some small things that we tend to overlook contain big things, including these items:

1. Small offerings: A friend of mine once gave two cents in an offering (all that he had), but within that two cents was a two thousand dollar blessing that God gave him in return.

2. Helping others get out of debt: By tithing on the amount of your newly defeated debt, God will help you pay off your other debts (e.g., pay off a $100 per month bill, then sow 10 percent of the paid bill into the lives of others to pay off their debt). By helping (watering) them, God helps (water) you (see Prov. 11:24-25).

3. Carrying your lunch to work: You may see this as only $5 a day (a small thing), but it's $25 a

week, $100 a month, or $1200 a year (a big thing). If you invest this $100 per month, in ten years this small thing will be worth $20,484 (a big thing), assuming a 10 percent return.

Principle #51

"Procrastination chains you to your present as your future moves past you."

Promise

He that gathereth in the summer is a wise son: but he that sleepeth in harvest is a son that causeth shame (Proverbs 10:5).

Power

Procrastination keeps us in the current situations that we hate as opportunity after opportunity pass us by. Each opportunity is calling us to move into the future where the victory over our present condition is waiting. Doing nothing is a sign that we accept our present situation. We tell ourselves that tomorrow we will start our budget, call the creditors, seek financial counsel, or stop using credit cards; but that tomorrow never comes. With each passing day, the sense of urgency subsides, and years later, we realize that our situation has only grown worse. The best time to move forward is when we first see the need. If we do not act then, it may never happen. These are some examples of the costs of procrastination:

1. By waiting five years to buy insurance, the monthly cost increases $15 per month or $3600 over 20 years.
2. If your goal is to save $100,000 by age 65, the required monthly investment will be $17.88 if you start saving at age 25, but $48.10 if you wait until age 35 to start saving.
3. By waiting 5 years to start saving $100 per month, you lose $56,000 over 20 years.

Why do people procrastinate?

Reason	How to Overcome This
• Fear of failure	• Meditate on the possibilities
• The task seems too big	• Break it down into smaller parts
• Don't know what to do or how to do it	• Obtain wise counsel

You must live with a sense of urgency.

Principle #52

"Only the Lord's architecture is built to handle the quakes and storms of life."

Promise

Whosoever cometh to Me, and heareth My sayings, and doeth them, I will show you to whom he is like: He is like a man which built an house, and digged deep, and laid the foundation on a rock: and when the flood arose, the stream beat vehemently upon that house, and could not shake it: for it was founded upon a rock (Luke 6:47-48).

Power

Many times Christians just do what *works* and not what the *Word* requires. What works normally seems fine until it's tested by the difficulties of life. Living on two incomes works fine until one income is lost due to downsizing; likewise, living from payday to payday without saving anything works until an emergency arises for which there is no spare money to handle it. What had appeared to work no longer does because its foundation was not the Word of God; therefore, God was not watching over it to perform it. The Word works, regardless of the economic times.

Principle #53

"Obedience to the Word of God is never a risk."

Promise

And Peter answered Him and said, Lord, if it be Thou, bid me come unto Thee on the water. And He said, Come. And when Peter was come down out of the ship, he walked on the water, to go to Jesus (Matthew 14:28-29).

Power

The will of God is His Word. Any time you obey His Word, the risk factor for failure is eliminated because God "hastens" (watches) His Word to perform it (see Jer. 1:12). From the world's perspective, it may appear risky; but God's Word never returns to Him void or without accomplishing that which He desires it to do (see Is. 55:11).

Actions that Appear Risky to the World	The Word
• Paying tithes and offerings when you're in need	• Malachi 3:11
• Helping others get out of debt when you're in debt	• Proverbs 11:24-25
• Living within one income	• Proverbs 31; Titus 2:3-5
• Paying your bills on time, even if your family has to do without some basic things	• Proverbs 3:27; Ecclesiastes 5:5
• Saving something every payday before you buy anything for yourself	• Proverbs 21:20 TLB

Principle #54

"God judges what you give by what you keep."

Promise

And He said, Of a truth I say unto you, that this poor widow hath cast in more than they all: For all these have of their abundance cast in unto the offerings of God: but she of her penury hath cast in all the living that she had (Luke 21:3-4).

Power

People base their giving on the amount that they give, while God bases our giving on what we have to give. (We cannot give our bill money because, to God, that belongs to someone else). Our willingness to give (see 2 Cor. 8:12) is more important to God than the amount we give. For if God sees in our heart the willingness to give, He will soon put it in our hand so that we may give it. Remember, we can only give what we have, and that's how God judges our giving.

Principle #55

"A bill that's unprepared for will always be unexpected."

Promise

A prudent man foreseeth the evil, and hideth himself: but the simple pass on, and are punished (Proverbs 22:3).

Power

We often use the excuse that an unexpected bill came from nowhere and threw off our budget. The truth is that very few bills are unexpected; they are just unprepared for. If we take the time to consider past and future events, most (if not all) needs can be foreseen before they happen, allowing us to set aside money today. Here is a list of some things that we can expect in life:

1. Illness/doctor visits
2. Church obligations
3. Car repairs
4. Car insurance
5. Holidays and birthdays
6. Home repairs
7. Taxes
8. School activities
9. Vacation
10. College education

Principle #56

"If you give what you don't need, you'll reap what you can't use."

Promise

Be not deceived; God is not mocked: for whatsoever a man soweth, that shall he also reap. For he that soweth to his flesh shall of the flesh reap corruption; but he that soweth to the Spirit shall of the Spirit reap life everlasting (Galatians 6:7-8).

Power

A sacrificial offering is something of value to you that you present as an offering unto God. The sacrifice must be *yours*, not a vendor's or creditor's (in reference to bill money). If you always give God an offering that you can afford, you will usually reap from God the things that you cannot use. That is, if you give something that is not important to you, you will harvest something that is useless, insignificant, and meaningless. (See Malachi 1.) Like a rubber band, giving is designed to stretch us at times or to pull us back so that we may be launched forward.

Principle #57

"Your giving and faith should be identical twins—conceived at the same time, growing at the same pace."

Promise

Therefore, as ye abound in every thing, in faith, and utterance, and knowledge, and in all diligence, and in your love to us, see that ye abound in this grace also (2 Corinthians 8:7).

Power

As a Christian, the Bible challenges us to grow (or increase) in spiritual matters such as faith, the Word, and love. However, just as important is the challenge from the Word to increase our giving. One of the financial goals Christians should establish is to increase their giving to their local church each year so that their giving and faith will reflect one another.

Principle #58

"The cry of the flesh should never be louder than the whisper of the Spirit."

Promise

And He said, Go forth, and stand upon the mount before the Lord. And, behold, the Lord passed by, and a great and strong wind rent the mountains, and brake in pieces the rocks before the Lord; but the Lord was not in the wind: and after the wind an earthquake; but the Lord was not in the earthquake: and after the earthquake a fire; but the Lord was not in the fire: and after the fire a still, small voice (1 Kings 19:11-12).

Power

The flesh, like hell and destruction, will never be satisfied, for its thirst cannot be quenched (see Prov. 27:20). The flesh will never tell you to spend less, but will tell you to make more to spend more. This is why as Christians we must seek and hear from the Holy Spirit before we buy anything. The Holy Spirit will speak softly, yet firmly, to you concerning a purchase. He will ask you to consider questions like:

1. Have you paid your tithe and offering?
2. Does this purchase reflect the character of God?
3. Have you paid your bills and put away savings?
4. If you can afford it, why charge it?
5. Does it fit comfortably into your budget?
6. Did you discuss it first with your spouse or covenant partner?
7. Does it help you to meet your goals?
8. Have you counted all the costs?

Beware: Excitement tries to drown the voice of the Holy Spirit! While the Holy Spirit gives you practical things to consider, the flesh pushes you to buy something just because your neighbors have it, because it's new, or for whatever reason. We tend to listen to our flesh because its says, "buy it now," which is what we want to hear. Be led by the Spirit so you can deny the lust of the flesh.

Principle #59

"As a mirror reflects a man's face, a checkbook reflects his priorities."

Promise

A good man's earnings advance the cause of righteousness. The evil man squanders his on sin (Proverbs 10:16 TLB).

Power

If you want to know what a person's priorities are, look at the way he spends money. A person may say, "I love God" or "I want to be debt free," but his checkbook may declare otherwise, revealing that he puts clothes, food, jewelry, and recreation before God or defeating indebtedness. A Christian's checkbook should show a strong commitment to advancing the Kingdom (tithes/offerings), eliminating debt, paying bills on time, and saving for his family's future over anything else. What does your checkbook say about you?

Principle #60

"Obstacles are situations that cause you to find a creative solution."

Promise

And when they could not come nigh unto Him for the press, they uncovered the roof where He was: and when they had broken it up, they let down the bed wherein the sick of the palsy lay (Mark 2:4).

Power

Every problem usually has various solutions. Consider, for every *problem* there's a *promise* that contains a *principle* that can lead to your *provision*. Whenever you have a financial problem, do the following:

1. Consult God and His Word for direction and creative ideas.
2. List all the possible options you've discovered and consider the pros and cons of each.
3. Consult your spouse/covenant partner for insight.
4. Discuss the problem and the possibilities with wise counsel, obtaining the benefit of his or her insight, advice, and experience.
5. Update and enhance your list of options based on their ideas.
6. Discuss all ideas with your spouse/covenant partner; put them in the order of priority.
7. Just do it!

Principle #61

"Discipline is the bridge that connects the unsuccessful to the road of success."

Promise

He openeth also their ear to discipline, and commandeth that they return from iniquity. If they obey and serve Him, they will spend their days in prosperity, and their years in pleasures (Job 36:10-11).

Power

Discipline is the ability to do what you don't enjoy to create what you love. It says, "I'll prepare a budget, track spending, cut costs, or balance the checkbook to achieve my goals of being debt-free, of having extra money, or of being current on my bills." Discipline starts by taking the time to develop a financial plan and then doing it. *Discipline understands that the benefits of having exceed the cost of getting.* To get to the road of success, this bridge must be crossed.

Principle #62

"The breeze that blows your money away may be coming from Heaven."

Promise

Ye looked for much, and, lo, it came to little; and when ye brought it home, I did blow upon it. Why? saith the Lord of hosts. Because of Mine house that is in waste, and ye run every man unto his own house (Haggai 1:9).

Power

Whenever believers lack or appear to have lost money, their first response is, "The devil came and took it"; however, that is not always the case. At times, God is behind our money leak or disappearance because we neglect the upkeep of His house to provide for our own. "Priority Spending" always instructs us to pay our tithe and offerings first, so that God's house is taken care of. Then He promises to take care of ours.

Principle #63

"Your greatest financial battle will be the one that you fight against yourself."

Promise

I know that good does not live in me—that is, in my human nature. For even though the desire to do good is in me, I am not able to do it (Romans 7:18 TEV).

Power

We, not the devil, are our own biggest obstacles. Jesus has already defeated the devil for us. *We don't need deliverance; we need discipline!* Once we overcome ourselves and live a disciplined life (e.g., stop going to malls, prepare and follow a budget, attack debt, learn more about finances), the battle will be won. The following are some basic steps to financial discipline:

1. Become accountable to someone who walks in victory and will challenge you to do the same!
2. Develop a standard time to review your finances, using a predetermined list of things to do. Do this with a friend.
3. Understand that your present financial situation does not reflect the character of God.
4. Understand that *doing nothing worsens your financial situation.*

Principle #64

"Understand it before you *undertake* it."

Promise

The simple believeth every word: but the prudent man looketh well to his going (Proverbs 14:15).

Power

If you don't understand a financial transaction well enough to explain it to someone else so he can understand it, you don't understand it well enough to spend God's money! Without understanding, it's impossible to determine what is a good move and what isn't. Even though the sales person understands it and is excited about it, you must do more research and obtain wise counsel so that *you* completely understand it. Don't buy anything until you do.

Principle #65

"God will never put in your hand what's not in your heart."

Promise

And she said, Oh my lord, as thy soul liveth, my lord, I am the woman that stood by thee here, praying unto the Lord. For this child I prayed; and the Lord hath given me my petition, which I asked of Him (1 Samuel 1:26-27).

Power

Like your electric company, God will only supply according to the demand. Though the electric company has the supply, it's only released when the demand is there. You must have a vision and a plan of what you want and how you'll use it for His glory. Once God sees the vision, He'll make the provision.

Principle #66

"Budgeting: Out-of-bounds lines designed to keep your scoring drive alive."

Promise

For which of you, intending to build a tower, sitteth not down first, and counteth the cost, whether he have sufficient enough to finish it? (Luke 14:28)

Power

A budget is not designed to restrain you, but rather to control cost and eliminate waste so that you will have more money left to achieve your life goals. A budget also serves the following purposes:

1. To give you an advanced spending plan.
2. To help you keep your bills less than your income.
3. To help you better understand your finances so that you can make more informed decisions.
4. To bring order to your life, for with order comes peace. (See Appendix I.)

Principle #67

"When your outflow exceeds your income, your upkeep becomes your downfall."

Promise

Much food is in the tillage of the poor: but there is that is destroyed for want of judgment (Proverbs 13:23).

Power

The problem is not that you don't make enough money, but that through poor money management you've spent more than you've made. The solution is to:

1. Develop a biblically based budget to limit and control your spending.
2. Reduce your consumption. Remember that a decrease in your consumption means an increase in your capital.

Don't run out and get a part-time job. If you get a job without obtaining discipline, you'll make more, spend more, and become more frustrated.

Principle #68

"Goals are like eyeglasses; they help to give focus to your vision."

Promise

Where there is no vision, the people perish: but he that keepeth the law, happy is he (Proverbs 29:18).

Power

Goals help you to stay focused and allow you to see things that are far off *now* but are forthcoming in your future. In addition, they help you to focus on what is *important* versus what's *interesting*. Often, it is the interesting things that rob you of your God-given purpose. Where there are no goals, your vision becomes blurred, causing you to be distracted by present-day events at the expense of future goals. This kills your motivation and easily leads you astray.

Principle #69

"The best person to handle finances is the person who can handle finances best."

Promise

From whom the whole body fitly joined together and compacted by that which every joint supplieth, according to the effectual working in the measure of every part, maketh increase of the body unto the edifying of itself in love (Ephesians 4:16).

Power

God hasn't necessarily called men to handle the family finances, but he has called men to provide them. Providing may mean working, establishing goals, and monitoring the finances, whether you or your spouse is handling them (e.g., writing checks, balancing the checkbook, making investments, etc.). Men, if your wife possesses the anointing to handle the finances, allow her to do it. No one has to know, all they will know is that your family is blessed. Every person has specific roles that help the body stay healthy, growing, and financially prosperous. Only when each person is working and functioning in his or her proper place can the body fully mature and reach its financial potential. Remember, regardless of your role in the finances, every joint is important.

Principle #70

"Debt never says, *spend less*; it always says, *make more!*"

Promise

Hell and destruction are never full; so the eyes of man are never satisfied (Proverbs 27:20).

Power

Debt is constantly fueled by the fleshly desire for more things! Your flesh, regardless of what you purchase, can never be satisfied. Thus, the voice of debt urges you to make more money in an attempt to satisfy its desires. Making more only increases debt's appetite and drive to spend more money. The best way to control and begin to eliminate debt is to spend less! Once you've become disciplined to spend less, then you can consider ways to make more. With discipline, this extra money will help you attack debt, not feed it.

Principle #71

"People who *see* 'nothing' *do* 'nothing' and therefore *have* 'nothing'."

Promise

Where there is no vision, the people perish: but he that keepeth the law, happy is he (Proverbs 29:18).

Power

What you see in your financial future will determine what you do; and what you do will determine what you have. Every action first starts as a thought. Consider Hebrews 11:17-19. Abraham was willing to sacrifice Isaac because he saw Isaac being raised from the dead, even before the preparation of the sacrifice. The focus of your mind determines both where you are now and where you are headed.

Principle #72

"Savings tell God that you have seed available to advance the Kingdom."

Promise

The good man's earnings advance the cause of righteousness. The evil man squanders his on sin (Proverbs 10:16 TLB).

Power

A pattern of saving has a variety of purposes, all of which are to glorify God. Savings can be used for emergencies, generational inheritances, helping those in need (not in greed!), enhancing your standard of living without having to incur debt, and, most importantly, advancing God's Kingdom. When we look at our savings, we must be able to say, "God, it's available to You. You gave it to me, and if I sow it, You'll return it to me." Special projects may be a time of special sowing. Savings can be one of the sources.

Principle #73

"The only way to get your money from the devil is to show God that you can handle it."

Promise

...the wealth of the sinner is laid up for the just (Proverbs 13:22).

Power

Why does the sinner have your money, and why do you rejoice in proclaiming this? Why are you so happy that someone else (and the wicked at that!) has your money? When are you going to get it? The wicked hold your money in a trust fund, controlling it and limiting your access to it until you meet specific conditions and reach maturity! God will transfer this wealth to you only after He sees you managing your present assets based on His principles in the Bible. He waits to see that you can properly handle it. Although it's easy to say, "I can handle it," God bases His outflow of blessings to you on how well you apply biblical principles to that which you already have.

Principle #74

"An excited customer will usually miss the bargain."

Promise

Ponder the path of thy feet, and let all thy ways be established (Proverbs 4:26).

Power

Never buy anything when you are excited! When excited, people usually don't think wisely concerning other options, bills that are due, goals, and vision. Before buying, prayerfully consider the consequences and match the spending up with your budget.

Warning: Most debt is accumulated when you are excited.

Principle #75

"Poverty is where ignorance and lack of discipline intersect."

Promise

My people are destroyed for a lack of knowledge (Hosea 4:6a).

Power

Poverty has very little to do with how much you make. It occurs when individuals don't take the time to learn about financial matters like insurance, debt elimination, taxes, etc. What people don't know creeps into financial situations and connects with a lack of discipline, thus creating poverty. Poverty is a lot like AIDS; it is an involuntary consequence from what is many times a voluntary decision and action. People choose to be in poverty because they refuse to educate themselves, discipline themselves, and sacrifice unnecessary desires to achieve the goal of prosperity. The number one goal of the disease of poverty is to make prosperity appear unattainable and to make it a desire, not a goal. *Remember, lack of knowledge plus lack of discipline equals lack of money!*

Principle #76

"You can't produce a different product by following the same process."

Promise

For if the first covenant had been faultless, then should no place have been sought for the second. ... In that He saith, A new covenant, He hath made the first one old. Now that which decayeth and waxeth old is ready to vanish away (Hebrews 8:7,13).

Power

You can't expect to change your current financial situation if you continue in your present habits. It should be obvious that what you're doing in your finances isn't working. To produce a different product (i.e., paying bills on time, accumulating savings, paying cash for items versus using a charge card), you must change the process that you're using. For instance, consider implementing a budget, cutting up some of your credit cards, obtaining wise counsel, learning more about finances, planning ahead, or creating some written goals. For every new procedure you implement in your life, you will discover or receive a new product!

Principle #77

"For every *problem*, God has given a *promise* that is linked to a *principle*, which leads to a *provision*."

Promise

There hath no temptation taken you but such as is common to man: but God is faithful, who will not suffer you to be tempted above that ye are able; but will with the temptation also make a way to escape, that ye may be able to bear it (1 Corinthians 10:13).

Power

God is aware of every financial problem before you encounter it. Because others have gone through the same situations, rest assured that wise counsel based on experience is available to help you get through the same thing. God's pattern is simple:

Process

Plan

- List your *problem*.
- Locate the *promise* that deals with your problem.
- From the promise, determine the *principle* (application).

- Debt
- 2 Kings 4:1-7

- Obtain wise counsel (v. 2a)
  Use all your resources (v. 2b)
  Get the family involved (v. 4)
  Follow a plan from wise counsel (v. 3-6),
  Use the extra money only for the debt.
  When the loan is paid off, don't get back into debt (v. 7)

- After the principle is practiced, God must *provide*. (The need of the woman in Second Kings 4 was more than met.)

Principle #78

"Every loan should have the flexibility to be bent into a gift."

Promise

Be not thou one of them that strike hands, or of them that are sureties for debts. If thou hast nothing to pay, why should he take away thy bed from under thee? (Proverbs 22:26-27)

Power

You should never loan money to someone or obtain a loan for someone if you can't afford to forfeit the money or repay the loan in the event that they don't repay it. If you ever decide to co-sign for someone, you must be able to repay the full amount yourself based on your budget. If the loan payment doesn't fit into your budget, you shouldn't co-sign for the loan, since you'll have to pay if the other person doesn't.

Principle #79

"Before Jesus paid the cost, He first counted it."

Promise

For which of you, intending to build a tower, sitteth not down first, and counteth the cost, whether he have sufficient to finish it? (Luke 14:28)

Power

Before you buy anything, count the entire cost that is involved. The purchase price is not the only cost incurred. There is also an operating and maintenance cost. If the total cost is not counted, you may be buying something that you can't afford. Consider the following example: You want to buy a $20,000 car with a $350 monthly payment, which you are prepared and equipped to handle. However, if you are like many people, you may fail to count the following costs that are related to the car's purchase: miles per gallon, type of gas required, cost of insurance, cost and frequency of repair, cost of routine maintenance (i.e., oil changes, new tires, tune-ups, etc.), resale value, and interest rates. These expenses could drive the actual monthly cost up to $500 per month, which may not fit comfortably into your budget.

Be sure to count all costs before you pay the price.

Principle #80

"When your financial habits change, so does the season of your life."

Promise

To every thing there is a season, and a time to every purpose under the heaven (Ecclesiastes 3:1).

Power

Your habits determine your financial strength (or lack), as well as the season you've chosen to live in. Remember, seasons can change. Here are the three most common financial seasons and the habits associated with each:

1. Egypt (*Not enough*)
   - Has no budget
   - Buys on impulse
   - Is proud and won't ask for help
   - Thinks things can't change
   - Pays tithe and offerings only when there is extra money
   - Pays bills after buying for self
   - Eats out often
   - Tolerates debt, even if minimum payment can't be made
   - Doesn't work with spouse/covenant partner
   - Tries to impress others
   - Refuses to learn about money
   - Loves name brands
2. Wilderness (*Just enough*)
   - Follows an unwritten budget
   - Accepts debt as long as minimum payment can be made
   - Pays tithe and offerings after paying other bills

- Fails to develop a comprehensive debt reduction plan
- Reads about financial strategies but never implements them
- Does little planning
- Lacks well-defined goals
- Is satisfied with salary versus income

3. Canaan Land (*More than enough*)
   - Recognizes the Word of God, not feelings or impulses, as the final authority that governs all finances
   - Sows into the lives of others
   - Pays bills on time, recognizing that his or her name affects God's name
   - Always works with spouse/covenant partner
   - Reviews finances regularly
   - Takes ownership for present and future financial status
   - Spends money as if it belongs to God
   - Obtains wise counsel
   - Is willing to sacrifice
   - Is organized and creative
   - Has well-defined goals
   - Pays tithe and offerings first; gives sacrificial offerings from surplus income, not income needed to pay bills
   - Attacks debt because it's an enemy; uses a credit card very rarely
   - Bases spending on goals and vision
   - Understands that he or she is blessed to be a blessing
   - Is always open to new ideas—even looks for them
   - Teaches his or her children about money
   - Plans ahead
   - Monitors spending in comparison to their budget
   - Sows and saves more as he makes more
   - Is a hard worker
   - Develops and follows a financial plan
   - Lives within one income

Principle #81

"There's a difference between being poor and being poor-minded."

Promise

For as he thinketh in his heart, so is he (Proverbs 23:7).

Power

Poverty is a disease of the mind, having very little to do with the size of your bank account. Vision is the antibiotic for the disease of poverty. A poor person, although he doesn't presently have extra money, can have the mind, the vision, the discipline, and the knowledge to turn his mess into a miracle. A poor-minded person says, "I can't have, I won't have, and I don't know if I should have what I need." The poor-minded person doesn't want help; he wants a handout.

Principle #82

"Don't let the goal of perfection rob you of the grounds of progress."

Promise

And let us not be weary in well doing: for in due season we shall reap, if we faint not (Galatians 6:9).

Power

You may not be able to do everything now, but you can do something! You must see the many steps involved in attaining your goal. Never get your steps and your goal confused, but in moving toward your goal be sure to recognize the progress that you have made. Completing each step is a requirement for reaching your goal. For example, bricks are not a house, but when they are brought together with other building materials and the effort of construction, they produce a house. Your goal may not be to build a house but to get out of debt. Consider the following steps for achieving this goal:

1. Pay your bills on time.
2. Stop using credit cards and other debt-producing devices.
3. Catch up on past-due bills.
4. Develop a balanced budget.
5. Write down a list of goals, a procedure for spending, and a clear reason for wanting to get out of debt.

Principle #83

"Vision is the gap that separates employers and employees."

Promise

The soul of the sluggard desireth, and hath nothing: but the soul of the diligent shall be made fat (Proverbs 13:4).

Power

The major difference between an employer and an employee is not money, for your boss very likely did not have much money when he first began. However, your contribution to the business is what helped to generate capital. The difference is vision. Your employer sees in you the God-given potential that you don't see in yourself. Regardless of your wage, your boss is making a profit from *your* potential that is at least four times as much as you make. Expand your vision about yourself! *Remember, if you're not the means of production, you're the tool of production.*

Principle #84

"Money is like a married woman; if the husband handles her properly, she has the ability to reproduce."

Promise

Let the earth bring forth grass, the herb yielding seed, and the fruit tree yielding fruit after his kind, whose seed is in itself, upon the earth: and it was so. And the earth brought forth grass, and herb yielding seed after his kind, and the tree yielding fruit, whose seed was in itself, after his kind... (Genesis 1:11-12).

Power

Money is designed by God to reproduce after its own kind. When it fails to do this, it has not fulfilled its purpose (see Mt. 25:14-30). When we (especially men) properly handle money based on God's instruction (budgeting, paying bills on time, giving tithes and offerings, saving, etc.), our money will reproduce. You need your money to reproduce so that:

1. You can advance God's Kingdom and establish His covenant.
2. You can provide for your family (even your extended family).
3. You can leave an inheritance to future generations.
4. You can be a blessing by helping others.
5. You can provide for God's house (your local church).
6. You can do the things you want to do.

It takes a lot of seed to do what God has called us to do.

Principle #85

"A wise man always lets others pay for his education."

Promise

I went by the field of the slothful, and by the vineyard of the man void of understanding; And, lo, it was all grown over with thorns, and nettles had covered the face thereof, and the stone wall thereof was broken down. Then I saw, and considered it well: I looked upon it, and received instruction (Proverbs 24:30-32).

Power

Experience is not always the best teacher. Do you need to experience financial hardship to know that it will destroy your marriage? Look at what it's done to others and learn from their example. Find people who are failing financially (it's not hard to do) and learn from them. List the mistakes they've made that are creating problems for them and vow not to duplicate them! Learn what they've done and be careful not to do the same.

Principle #86

"Salary is the greatest enemy of income."

Promise

Drink waters out of thine own cistern, and running waters out of thine own well. Let thy fountains be dispersed abroad, and rivers of water in the streets. Let them be only thine own, and not strangers' with thee (Proverbs 5:15-17).

Power

The average person is worth *at least* four times what he makes. A salary may keep a person content and pacified; therefore, only those with a passion to tap all their potential can graduate to an income. Income comes only when you are paid what you're worth. An income is based on what you're worth, while a salary is based on what others think you're worth. Consider what business opportunity you can begin (with careful planning) so that you can move from a salary (limited) to an income (unlimited).

Principle #87

"The best medicine for marriage is a balanced budget."

Promise

A merry heart doeth good like a medicine: but a broken spirit drieth the bones (Proverbs 17:22).

Power

The root of most marital problems is monetarily based. *Bringing order to your finances will help bring order to your marriage.* Organizing your finances can be broken down into the following basic steps:

1. Decide what you value in life.
2. Allow your values to birth your goals.
3. List what you must do (your objectives) to attain each goal.
4. Develop a family budget that is driven by the family's agreed-upon goals.
5. Follow your budget.
6. Review your finances together regularly.
7. Become accountable to another couple.

Principle #88

"Greed wants you to look successful before you are successful."

Promise

Hell and destruction are never full; so the eyes of man are never satisfied (Proverbs 27:20).

Power

Greedy people will lie and tell you to "fake it until you make it." It is not the will of God that we as believers try to impress people with designer clothes, expensive jewelry, or fancy cars, giving the appearance that we're blessed before the manifestation of the blessing. Buy only what you know you can afford.

Principle #89

"Whatever God gives you will require His help to keep it."

Promise

The blessing of the Lord, it maketh rich, and He addeth no sorrow with it (Proverbs 10:22).

Power

Whatever you receive from God came according to His purpose and His will for your life. If you needed God to get the blessing, you also need Him to keep it. The spirit of possession is what God wants from believers. If and when the Blesser leaves, so does the blessing. Remember, anything that makes God unnecessary is unnecessary.

Principle #90

"Nothing is too difficult if it can be broken down into bite-sized, believable pieces."

Promise

Though thy beginning was small, yet thy latter end shall greatly increase (Job 8:7).

Power

Many times people don't attempt something because the task seems too overwhelming. The solution is to divide the task into smaller, believable pieces. This is illustrated in my "peanut butter and crackers" theory. How can you eat peanut butter crackers without a drink? You take one cracker at a time and divide it into small bites. The same theory applies to your finances. Try the following to get you started:

1. List all your financial problems.
2. Prioritize them.
3. Understand each problem and look for possible solutions.
4. Start working with the first problem, using your solutions.

Principle #91

"Prosperity is something that is often displayed but never advertised."

Promise

They that trust in their wealth, and boast themselves in the multitude of their riches; None of them can by any means redeem his brother, nor give to God a ransom for him (Psalm 49:6-7).

Power

Never boast about what you have; let it speak for itself. When God prospers you, He will announce it to other people for His glory. Your prosperity is proof that the things you teach, profess, and speak work; and it is designed to give hope to the hopeless and to provide a testimony to empower you for future circumstances.

Principle #92

"You can tell what God trusts you with by what you have; and you can tell what you trust God with by what you give."

Promise

Every man according as he purposeth in his heart, so let him give; not grudgingly, or of necessity: for God loveth a cheerful giver. And God is able to make all grace abound toward you; that ye, always having all sufficiency in all things, may abound to every good work: As it is written, He hath disbursed abroad; he hath given to the poor: his righteousness remaineth forever (2 Corinthians 9:7-9).

Power

Our level of giving is the meter that judges our trust in God. When we give, we give with the trust and assurance that God will return it to us when we need it. Likewise, when God gives us things, He trusts that we will keep and manage them according to His will and for His glory. God gives to us to the level that He can trust us to give back to Him (by way of the local church) when He needs the resources He has given us.

Principle #93

"When there is no emergency fund, everything becomes an emergency."

Promise

Go to the ant, thou sluggard; consider her ways, and be wise: Which having no guide, overseer, or ruler, Provideth her meat in the summer, and gathereth her food in the harvest. How long wilt thou sleep, O sluggard? when wilt thou arise out of thy sleep? Yet a little sleep, a little slumber, a little folding of the hands to sleep: So shall thy poverty come as one that travelleth, and thy want as an armed man (Proverbs 6:6-11).

Power

When no money has been set aside, the smallest financial problem causes the largest disturbance and creates more debt. A plan for potential problems must be made in advance, so that you can get through the problems with minimal difficulty (see Prov. 22:3). As you develop a plan, follow these or similar steps:

1. Develop an emergency fund. Commit to setting aside money every payday to fund this account. Don't touch it except for emergencies. (A clearance sale at the mall is not an emergency!) The goal should be to accrue savings equal to at least three months of living expenses.

2. Develop an emergency budget that outlines your potential reduced income. Then you will know how much must be cut from your expenses if you are to continue to live within your budget.

3. Outline which expenses you would reduce and how. Practice the plan at least twice a year to make sure that it works. Use this money to increase your emergency fund.

4. Identify which creditors will allow you to defer or reduce payments for a period of time due to hardships. Factor this information into number three.

Without an emergency fund, an emergency will cause you to:

1. Accumulate more debt to pay bills.

2. Get behind on bills and be pressured by creditors.

3. Become discouraged.

Your emergency plan must address death, disease, disability, downsizing, and disaster. (See Second Kings 4:1-7 and Nehemiah 5:1-5.)

Principle #94

"Your harvest is determined not only by how much seed is sown but also by how much seed is kept."

Promise

And He looked up, and saw the rich men casting their gifts into the treasury. And He saw also a certain poor widow casting in thither two mites. And He said, Of a truth I say unto you, that this poor widow hath cast in more than they all: For all these have of their abundance cast in unto the offerings of God: but she of her penury hath cast in all the living that she had (Luke 21:1-4).

Power

In determining your harvest, God not only considers what you've given, but just as importantly, what you've kept. God blesses based on comparison. He compares what you've given to what you've kept. By doing this, He determines the level of sacrifice.

Principle #95

"God is more concerned with your outcome than your income."

Promise

Remove far from me vanity and lies: give me neither poverty nor riches; feed me with food convenient for me: Lest I be full and deny Thee, and say, Who is the Lord? or lest I be poor, and steal, and take the name of my God in vain (Proverbs 30:8-9).

Power

Money is more important to us than it is to God. God will never allow His blessing (income) to negatively affect your outcome. He's more concerned about developing you to reach your God-given purpose than in just enriching you. Everyone's purpose does not require riches! God wants to give you exactly what you need to fulfill *His* purpose—no more, no less.

Principle #96

"Financial problems are not the result of the devil, but of bad decisions."

Promise

And when the woman saw that the tree was good for food, and that it was pleasant to the eyes, and a tree to be desired to make one wise, she took of the fruit thereof, and did eat, and gave also unto her husband with her; and he did eat (Genesis 3:6).

Power

As we go through financial difficulties, it's easier to say, "The devil is messing with my finances," than to admit, "I messed up my finances by my stupid decisions." In reality, most people's financial dilemmas are not a result of the devil, but rather, they are due to bad decisions that were not based on the Word. Such decisions include, but are not limited to:

1. Using your credit card instead of paying cash or waiting until you can pay cash for the purchase.
2. Not paying your tithe and offering.
3. Eating out instead of cooking on a regular basis.
4. Buying a new car when there is nothing wrong with the old one.
5. Quitting your job before you've secured another one.
6. Running up your phone bill instead of writing a letter.
7. Going shopping regularly.
8. Not paying your bills on time.

Principle #97

"If you don't *organize* your finances you'll *agonize* over them."

Promise

A land of darkness, as darkness itself; and of the shadow of death, without any order, and where the light is as darkness (Job 10:22).

Let all things be done decently and in order (1 Corinthians 14:40).

Power

When your finances are out of order, you don't have a clue as to your location, destination, or direction. For instance, it's like taking all the pages out of the phone book and scattering them across your room, creating a mess. When the pages were in order, you had a neat, packaged tool that could help fulfill a purpose. However, once its pages are disordered, the phone book no longer looks or performs like a phone book. The mess appears impossible to organize. So it is with your finances. To get organized, try the following ideas:

1. Get some manila folders.
2. List all your bills. Organize them based on the week that they are due. Label all folders according to the bills contained in them.
3. Locate all past due bills, organize them from smallest to largest, and place them in one folder. Call each creditor to discuss and set a payment plan for paying off the bill.

4. Organize all loan papers, contracts, and bank statements to keep track of your status and progress.

5. Plan your saving, investing, and use of tax refunds carefully. Let this money make money for you and create extra income.

6. Learn how to read and understand IRS policies and other legal papers so that you can use them to your advantage in preparing for the future.

7. Understand your company benefits and any titles to property you may hold. These assets are possible weapons against financial bondage.

8. Set goals and objectives to pay off your bills. Share your plan and your progress as a testimony to God's goodness and the benefits of being free of financial bondage to save, sow, and spend for His glory.

9. Be sure to check your credit report regularly. Understand and verify the accuracy of what it contains.

10. Prepare now for your death so that your family does not suffer. Make a will. Keep your insurance policies up to date.

11. Keep an updated "to do" list so that you always know where you stand and whether or not you are moving forward.

Principle #98

"Financial blueprints are useless if there is no contracted builder."

Promise

Lazy people want much but get little, while the diligent are prospering (Proverbs 13:4 TLB).

Power

What good is it to write out your goals and to have a plan, a confession, and a stated purpose if you don't execute them? You must be willing to take the written and make it a reality. Although many have dreams and aspirations, few are willing to move forward and possess them. Your goals are the plan that outlines the final appearance of the building.

Principle #99

"Frustration about your present financial situation creates either a catalyst for change or a cause for failure."

Promise

And they come unto Him, bringing one sick of the palsy, which was borne of four. And when they could not come nigh unto Him for the press, they uncovered the roof where He was: and when they had broken it up, they let down the bed wherein the sick of the palsy lay (Mark 2:3-4).

Power

Financial problems always cause frustration, but not all frustration is bad. Use your frustration to fuel your journey from where you are to where you want to be. Become so frustrated with your present financial situation that you start working to change it. A catalyst always causes a change, either slowing down a process or speeding it up. Allow your frustrations to slow down spending and speed up savings. If your frustration doesn't become your catalyst, it becomes your reason for failure.

Principle #100

"It's impossible to make the right financial decision with the wrong information."

Promise

What a shame—yes, how stupid!—to decide before knowing the facts (Proverbs 18:13 TLB).

Power

Before making a financial decision, take the time to obtain all the facts and information you need to make a wise decision. Review these carefully until you can explain them to someone else. Ask questions until you understand the information you have gathered. Consider all your options. Decisions made with wrong or partial information will result in poor financial decisions that will affect you for years. Get the facts before you spend the money, and be motivated by facts, not feelings.

Principle #101

"The miracle of provision is only the packaging of the message."

Promise

That they might set their hope in God, and not forget the works of God, but keep His commandments (Psalm 78:7).

Power

Every paid bill is a miracle from God due to His provision. However, we so often focus on the temporal miracle and miss the eternal message. The miracle is simply the details of a specific experience that reveals a larger picture with a more general principle. The eternal message is simple: If God provided for you in the past, He'll provide for you in the future, for He changes not. Make sure that you understand the message of your miracle.

Principle #102

"The only difference between debt and the devil is that the devil can't get any bigger."

Promise

Be sober, be vigilant; because your adversary the devil, as a roaring lion, walketh about, seeking whom he may devour (1 Peter 5:8).

The thief cometh not, but for to steal, and to kill, and to destroy: I am come that they might have life, and that they might have it more abundantly (John 10:10).

Power

Debt and the devil have many similarities; they both desire to kill, steal, and destroy. They will try to control and dominate your life, seeking to put you in bondage so that you cannot achieve or fulfill the will of God. *Jesus has already defeated the devil; but He left us with the responsibility of defeating debt.* Debt can and does get bigger daily through accruing interest. What started as a cute, easy-to-handle cub can become a lion that is poised and ready to destroy you. Always remember, interest grows daily; this includes interest on the interest as well as interest on the bill.

Principle #103

"Successful people do what others refuse to do."

Promise

The soul of the sluggard desireth, and hath nothing: but the soul of the diligent shall be made fat (Proverbs 13:4).

Power

Successful people determine to do whatever it takes, regardless of the sacrifice, to reach their goals. Compare the following:

Successful People	Unsuccessful People
• Develop and follow a budget	• Spend money until it's gone
• Review finances regularly	• Never review finances
• Ask questions, read financial info, and attend workshops	• Believe that they don't need to understand financial information
• Take time to develop detailed goals and objectives	• Dream about desires but set no plan
• Make financial sacrifices to achieve future goals	• Acquire everything now, when they want it

Principle #104

"The problem with debt is that it starts off as fun."

Promise

Choosing rather to suffer affliction with the people of God, than to enjoy the pleasures of sin for a season (Hebrews 11:25).

Power

No one intends to have uncontrollable debt. The reason debt entraps so many people is that it begins as fun. When you can use your credit card today and walk away with whatever is appealing to your flesh, you register very little emotional realization that you've just spent money that must be repaid tomorrow. This is true because no cash has exchanged hands. When, however, you "understand its end" (see Ps. 73:17) and see the large penalties you pay in interest charges and a high monthly statement, and in the problems it causes between you and your spouse, you suddenly realize that "the thrill is gone, baby!"

Principle #105

"The root of debt must be exposed before it can be attacked."

Promise

So the servants of the householder came and said unto him, Sir, didst not thou sow good seed in thy field? From whence then hath it tares? He said unto them, An enemy hath done this... (Matthew 13:27-28a).

Power

Destroy the root, and you will destroy the fruit. Before you can overcome any debt, you must understand how and why the debt was created. Each bill should be listed with a detailed explanation as to why it arose. Only then, when you see the root problem, can you eliminate the debt. Credit cards are a common root that most people are not willing to destroy; therefore the tree of debt will always bear fruit. Even though you may stop spending for a while, as long as the root exists, so will the potential to have the fruit. Other possible roots of debt include the following:

1. Going to malls.
2. Watching TV.
3. Socializing with friends who spend.
4. Having low self-esteem.
5. Trying to impress or compete with others.
6. Having wrong priorities.

Without addressing the root, you will repeat the debt cycle over and over again (see Prov. 26:11)!

Appendix A

The Ten-Ten Theory

Here are just a few strategies to cut your costs. By using these strategies to reduce ten expenses by at least ten dollars a month, your pot of oil will immediately yield $100 per month. By developing creative ways to cut your costs, you can save a lot of money and have fun in the process!

Strategy	Monthly Savings	Yearly Savings
1. Carry lunch and snacks to work. Eliminate eating out every day.	_____	_____
2. Locate the telephone company that has the lowest rates and bills on six-second intervals.	_____	_____
3. Eliminate unnecessary phone features such as call waiting, call return, caller ID, and three-way calling.	_____	_____
4. Create a good payment history; then ask your current credit card vendor to reduce your interest rate because of your payment record, or locate another vendor with better interest rates.	_____	_____
5. Eliminate ATM fees and non-sufficient-funds charges by balancing your checkbook.	_____	_____
6. Purchase life insurance through an insurance quote service.	_____	_____
7. Eliminate premium cable TV.	_____	_____

Strategy	Monthly Savings	Yearly Savings
8. Purchase clothes from an "upscale" consignment shop or buy irregulars (brand names).	_____	_____
9. Shop around and compare prices on car and homeowner insurance. Increase your deductible. Use brokers that write policies for several companies.	_____	_____
10. Purchase your checks from a discount check broker:	_____	_____

- Checks in the Mail (1-800-733-4443)
- Artistic Checks (1-800-244-7621).

Note: These are just a few ideas that you can possibly use to cut your expenses. Brainstorm with friends for additional ideas. Use all ideas to the fullest—the sky is the limit on how much fat you can cut from your expenditures.

Appendix B

Tax Tips

Here are some basic deductions that most people can take. Every dollar deducted saves you at least 15 cents in federal taxes.

1. IRA contributions
2. Non-cash gifts to charity (including your church)
3. Miles that you drive for charity (including services that you perform for your church)
4. Unreimbursed expenses you encounter for charity (e.g., church conventions)
5. Teaching and study materials (books, tapes, seminars, etc.) that help you to prepare to teach at your church
6. Home mortgage closing cost expenses that are itemized on your closing statement:
   - Points (you pay)
   - Interest
   - Prepaid taxes
   - Points (the seller pays)
7. Tax preparation fees
8. Unreimbursed job expenses
9. In-house child care wages
10. Miles driven for medical purposes

Appendix C

Possible Expenses and Priority of Spending

1. Tithes and offerings
2. Bills and necessary living expenses
   - Mortgage payment
   - Rent
   - Electricity
   - Water
   - Gas
   - Heating oil
   - Telephone
   - Groceries
   - Home maintenance
   - Ground care
   - Clothes/children's clothes
   - Medical, dental, and optical needs
   - Transportation (registration, gas, oil, tires, repair, etc.)
   - Insurance (auto, life, property, renter's, etc.)
   - Child Care (alimony, in-house child care wages, daycare, etc.)
   - Anniversary and birthday cards/gifts for spouse, children, and pastor
   - Business-related expenses (education, travel, etc.)
3. Savings
   - Regular
   - Retirement
   - Investment
   - College
   - Other
4. Non-Necessities
   - Dry cleaning

- Cable TV
- Business lunches
- Contributions to charities
- Birthday cards/gifts for friends
- Business-related gifts and donations
- Wedding and baby shower cards/gifts
- All recreation and entertainment, including vacations and travel for pleasure
- Personal items (beauty/barber shop, cosmetics and toiletries, pets, etc.)
- Household items (appliances, tools, linens, etc.)
- Children's allowances
- Newspapers and magazines
- Other

5. Wants and desires
   - Hobbies

Appendix D

Tapping Your Well for Extra Income
(To Accumulate Savings or Reduce Debt)

Strategy	Amount
1. Apply the Ten-Ten theory (see Appendix A).	_____
2. Use tax strategies to obtain larger refunds (Appendix B).	_____
3. Request refund of utility deposit plus interest after one year.	_____
4. Adjust your tax withholding (Form W-4) and get your refund now.	_____
5. Check with your state "eschews" department for unclaimed money that may be due you.	_____
6. Complete Form W-5 (Earned Income Credit), if eligible. Advance payment credit to your paycheck.	_____
7. Tap into the entire cash value of your whole life insurance policy.	_____
8. Request to work overtime; use the extra income wisely (e.g., pay off bills, increase savings, add money to emergency fund, etc).	_____
9. Utilize company benefits that make you money (e.g., 401k—your employer will match some, if not all that you save) and save you taxes (e.g., 401k, flex spending plan, medical reimbursements).	_____
10. Tap into your 401k to pay off higher interest rate debts and make a plan to repay what you borrow. (You would actually be borrowing from yourself and paying yourself back).	_____

Strategy	**Amount**
11. Convert your talents and hobbies into a business to provide cash.	_____
12. Sell or donate unused assets (e.g., clothes).	_____
13. Amend your tax return if deductions in Appendix B were overlooked.	_____
14. Get creditors to reduce the interest rate on your outstanding balance based on your good past payment history. Continue to make the same monthly payment at the lower interest rate to reduce the debt more quickly.	_____
15. Consider a part-time job. Use the extra money for a good purpose (e.g., pay off bills, increase savings, add money to emergency fund, etc.).	_____

Appendix E

How To Get Out of Debt and Stay Out

1. See debt as a hostile enemy in opposition to the will of God for your life.
2. Face your debt. You must face it before you can fix it (see Is. 17:24,32).
   - List all bills.
   - Admit that you have a problem.
3. Understand why each debt arose and learn from your mistake; if you don't, you'll repeat it (see Prov. 26:11; 24:30-32).
4. See the benefit of being debt free. The potential is greater than the problem.
   - When you can handle extra money, God (the king) will trust you with more money.
   - Becoming debt free will enhance your marriage (or bring release to marry).
   - You will have the ability to help your family (i.e., the family curse will be broken; you will be able to offer hope and money).
5. Become accountable to *someone*, but not just *anyone*. Choose someone you can trust in both character and relationship.
   - Open all your finances (everything) to your accountability partner.
   - Receive instruction from him or her (and follow it).
   - Let him or her be a positive example for you and teach you how to walk in victory.
   - Request that the person to whom you are accountable be firm and up front with you, keeping you honest and on target (see Prov. 28:23).

6. Destroy the root of the problem.
   - Cut up credit cards.
   - Close accounts.
   - Stop ATM use.
   - Stop seeing friends who do not encourage responsible spending.
   - Exchange poor lifestyle habits for those in keeping with your financial goals.
7. Operate on a cash-only basis. Don't use credit!
8. Control spending. Follow your budget.
9. Identify your weapons—"What has thou in the house?" (See Second Kings 4:2.) (Potential weapons are listed in Appendices A, B, and D.)
10. Lay out your plan, bill by bill. Show how each weapon will be used.
11. Attack! Be relentless! Once a bill is paid, use the additional money to pay off another bill.
12. Help someone else get out of debt.

Appendix F

Items for Sacrifice

1. Reduce the purchase of meat or other luxury items on your grocery list (e.g., ice cream, snack foods, convenience foods).
2. Eliminate perfume, fingernail polish, or other personal items for a month.
3. Skip a trip to the barber or beauty shop.
4. Cancel your newspaper subscription for a month.
5. Carry your lunch to work for a month.
6. Eliminate cable television for three months.
7. Don't buy any new clothes or jewelry for a month.
8. Eliminate extra, unnecessary phone features.
9. Do not make any long-distance calls for a month.
10. Give up your cellular phone.
11. Give up a meal or two (do more fasting).
12. Iron your shirt rather than taking it to the dry cleaner.
13. Reduce your family entertainment expenses by going to public facilities and events for entertainment and recreation.
14. Cut your own lawn and wash your own car.

Appendix G

Control Spending

1. Spend money as if it belongs to God.
2. Eliminate bad habits.
3. Follow your budget.
4. Arrange for direct deposit of your paycheck.
5. Establish clear goals and objectives.
6. Review spending to see if your expenditures help to achieve goals and objectives.
7. View your spouse as your teammate and work together.
8. Don't buy anything that you don't understand.
9. Become organized and be systematic in your payments and record keeping.
10. Destroy all credit and debit (ATM) cards. Keep one all-purpose card.
11. Deduct credit card charges in your checkbook as money is spent.
12. Make cost controlling and cutting a game: If you beat the budget, you get the extra money!
13. Let the "best" (most competent) person handle finances.
14. Establish a standard time to pay bills and discuss finances with your spouse/covenant partner.
15. Balance your checkbook.
16. Identify in advance what area you will cut when a sacrificial offering is required.

Appendix H

Rebuilding Your Credit

1. Review your credit record for errors and make sure that all information is accurate, current, and complete.
2. Have incorrect information removed from your record. Contact all three major bureaus and have information sent to all vendors who received files within the past six months.
3. Submit a letter of explanation for any negative records that were the result of unusual circumstances.
4. Negotiate pay-off terms with creditors. Request that they remove all negative information from your credit record. Get the agreed-upon terms in writing.
5. Always pay bills on time!
6. Obtain a secured loan using the bank's money and consistently pay it on time.
7. Obtain credit references that are viewed as "strong" (e.g., credit cards, bank loans).
8. Eliminate credit references that are viewed as "poor."
9. Develop a relationship with a banker. Explain your situation and plan to him or her.
10. Get caught up on all bills; they don't have to be paid off.
11. Once bills are current and you have been consistent in paying for three to six months, contact

     vendors with a brief but convincing reason to remove old information.

12. Don't apply for any new credit until old problems are resolved. Too many inquires are not good!

13. Dispute any questionable item. If the vendor doesn't respond within 30 days, it's automatically removed.

14. Request that vendors with whom you have a good payment record submit a note to the credit bureaus to be included in your file.

15. Get your vendors to revise your credit rating after a series of on-time payments.

Appendix I

Develop a Biblically Based Budget

1. Agree with your spouse/covenant partner to develop and follow a budget. (See Amos 3:3.)
2. Pray for God's direction and insight. (See Proverbs 3:5-6.)
3. Work with your spouse/covenant partner to develop the budget. (See Ecclesiastes 5:9-12.)
4. Identify your net income. Compare it with all your bills and living expenses (Appendix C). (See Luke 14:28.)
5. Develop "Spending Priorities"! Assign each item in your budget a "priority" code. Make sure that the top priority codes are always taken care of first (Appendix C)! (See Proverbs 3:9-10.)
6. Agree with your spouse/covenant partner on the actual numbers and the "priority" codes. (See Amos 3:3.)
7. Plan and include in the budget provision for future events, emergencies, and unforeseen expenses. (See Proverbs 22:3 TLB.)
8. Determine when bills will be due (Proverbs 3:27). List bills by week on the "Weekly Budget Plan" (Appendix J) so that bills are paid on time.
9. Follow your budget.
10. Review actual spending on a regular basis by category against the budget. (There should be only one checking account. See Habakkuk 2:2 and Proverbs 27:23 TLB.)

Appendix J

Weekly Budget Plan

Item	Due Date	1st-8th	9th-15th	16th-24th	25th-31st	Total
Net Income	_____	_____	_____	_____	_____	_____
Tithe	_____	_____	_____	_____	_____	_____
Offering	_____	_____	_____	_____	_____	_____
Housing	_____	_____	_____	_____	_____	_____
Water	_____	_____	_____	_____	_____	_____
Phone	_____	_____	_____	_____	_____	_____
Electricity	_____	_____	_____	_____	_____	_____
Food	_____	_____	_____	_____	_____	_____
Lunch	_____	_____	_____	_____	_____	_____
Entertainment	_____	_____	_____	_____	_____	_____
Clothes	_____	_____	_____	_____	_____	_____
Cleaning	_____	_____	_____	_____	_____	_____
Medical	_____	_____	_____	_____	_____	_____
Car Note	_____	_____	_____	_____	_____	_____
Gas	_____	_____	_____	_____	_____	_____
Insurance: Car	_____	_____	_____	_____	_____	_____
Personal	_____	_____	_____	_____	_____	_____
Life	_____	_____	_____	_____	_____	_____
Child Care	_____	_____	_____	_____	_____	_____
Savings	_____	_____	_____	_____	_____	_____
Maint.	_____	_____	_____	_____	_____	_____
Misc.	_____	_____	_____	_____	_____	_____
Total Disbursements	_____	_____	_____	_____	_____	_____
Excess	_____	_____	_____	_____	_____	_____

D *Destiny Image*
New Releases

WORSHIP: THE PATTERN OF THINGS IN HEAVEN
by Joseph L. Garlington.
Joseph Garlington, a favorite Promise Keepers' speaker and worship leader, delves into Scripture to reveal worship and praise from a Heaven's-eye view. Learn just how deep, full, and anointed God intends our worship to be.
ISBN 1-56043-195-4 $9.99p

WHEN GOD STRIKES THE MATCH
by Dr. Harvey R. Brown, Jr.
A noted preacher, college administrator, and father of an "all-American" family—what more could a man want? But when God struck the match that set Harvey Brown ablaze, it ignited a passion for holiness and renewal in his heart that led him into a head-on encounter with the consuming fire of God.
ISBN 0-7684-1000-2 $9.99p

THE LOST ART OF INTERCESSION
by Jim W. Goll.
How can you experience God's anointing power as a result of your own prayer? Learn what the Moravians discovered during their 100-year prayer Watch. They sent up prayers; God sent down His power. Jim Goll, who ministers worldwide through a teaching and prophetic ministry, urges us to heed Jesus' warning to "watch." Through Scripture, the Moravian example, and his own prayer life, Jim Goll proves that "what goes up must come down."
ISBN 1-56043-697-2 $9.99p

FOR GOD'S SAKE GROW UP!
by David Ravenhill.
It's time to grow up...so that we can fulfill God's purposes for us and for our generation! For too long we've been spiritual children clinging to our mother's leg, refusing to go to school on the first day. It's time to put away childish things and mature in the things of God—there is a world that needs to be won to Christ!
ISBN 1-56043-299-3 $9.99p

Available at your local Christian bookstore.

Internet: http://www.reapernet.com

Prices subject to change without notice.